NORTH DAKOTA

ALASKA

CANADA

PACIFIC
OCEAN

UNITED
STATES

HAWAII

PUERTO
RICO

MEXICO

NORTH DAKOTA

HELLO
U.S.A.

by Joan Marie Verba

Lerner Publications Company

You'll find this picture of wheat at the beginning of each chapter in this book. North Dakota produces more wheat than any other state except Kansas. Many farmers in North Dakota grow durum wheat, which is used to make pasta. In fact, North Dakota produces about 80 percent of all the durum wheat grown in the United States. That's enough to make 93 servings of pasta for each American.

Cover (left): Badlands and Little Missouri River. Cover (right): Sunflowers in a North Dakota field. Pages 2–3: Hayfield in the Red River Valley. Page 3: Downtown Fargo.

Copyright © 2003 by Lerner Publications Company

This book is available in two editions:
Library binding by Lerner Publications Company, a division of Lerner Publishing Group
Soft cover by First Avenue Editions, an imprint of Lerner Publishing Group
241 First Avenue North
Minneapolis, MN 55401 U.S.A.

Website address: www.lernerbooks.com

Library of Congress Cataloging-in-Publication Data

Verba, Joan Marie.
    North Dakota / by Joan Marie Verba. (Rev. and expanded 2nd ed.)
        p.   cm. — (Hello U.S.A.)
      Includes bibliographical references and index.
    Summary: An introduction to the geography, history, economy, people, environmental issues, and interesting sites of North Dakota.
      ISBN: 0–8225–4097–5 (lib. bdg. : alk paper)
      ISBN: 0–8225–0790–0 (pbk. : alk. paper)
      1. North Dakota—Juvenile literature. [1. North Dakota.] I. Title.
    II. Series.
    F636.3.V47 2003
    978.4—dc21   2001007214

Manufactured in the United States of America
1 2 3 4 5 6 – JR – 08 07 06 05 04 03

CONTENTS

Sunflowers are one of North Dakota's main agricultural products.

THE LAND

Plain and Plateau

Some people think of North Dakota as an empty, flat land. But there is more to the state than silent grasslands. People who get to know North Dakota will discover scenic lakes and rivers, rolling hills, and colorful plant and animal life.

North Dakota is a midwestern state, lying between Canada to the north and South Dakota directly to the south. On the east, the Red River separates North Dakota from Minnesota. To the west is Montana.

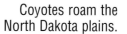
Coyotes roam the
North Dakota plains.

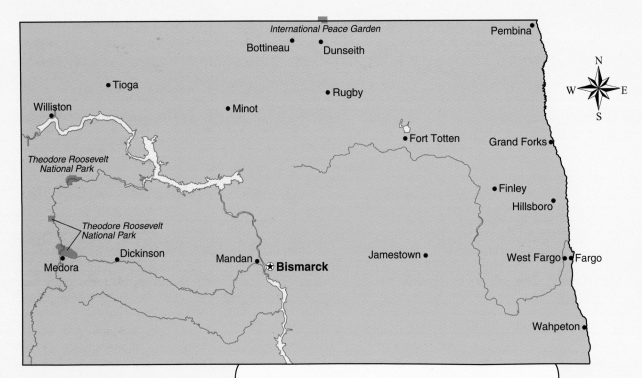

International Peace Garden

Pembina

Bottineau • • Dunseith

• Tioga

• Rugby

Williston •

• Minot

Theodore Roosevelt
National Park

• Fort Totten

Grand Forks •

• Finley

Hillsboro •

Theodore Roosevelt
National Park

• Dickinson

Mandan • • ★ **Bismarck**

Jamestown •

West Fargo • • Fargo

Medora

Wahpeton •

N

W ✦ E

S

The drawing of North Dakota on this page is called a political map. It shows features created by people, including cities, railways, and parks. The map on the facing page is called a physical map. It shows physical features of North Dakota, such as mountains, rivers, and lakes. The colors represent a range of elevations, or heights above sea level (see legend box). This map also shows the geographical regions of North Dakota.

NORTH DAKOTA
Political Map

★ State capital

0   20   40 Miles

0   20   40   60   80 Kilometers

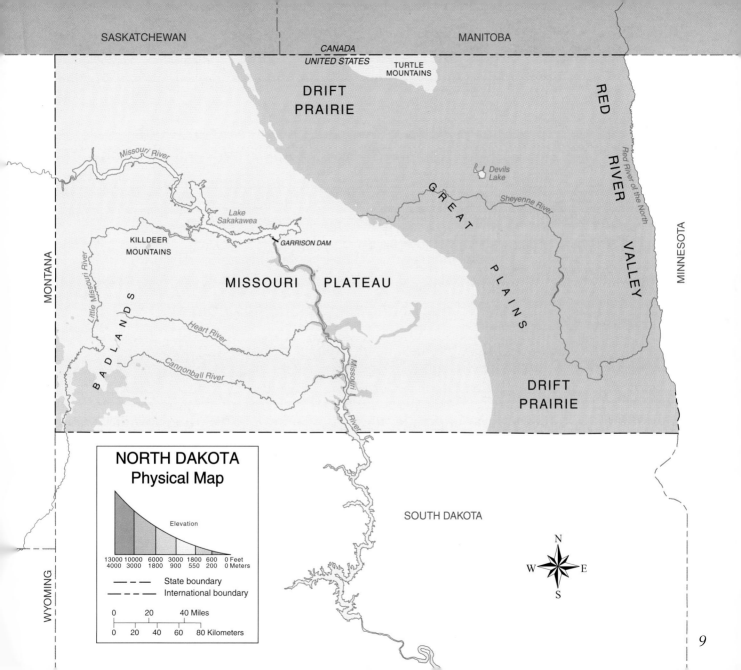

SASKATCHEWAN

MANITOBA

CANADA
UNITED STATES

TURTLE
MOUNTAINS

DRIFT
PRAIRIE

RED

RIVER

Red River of the North

Missouri River

Devils
Lake

G
R
E
A
T

Sheyenne River

VALLEY

MONTANA

Lake
Sakakawea

KILLDEER
MOUNTAINS

GARRISON DAM

MISSOURI   PLATEAU

P
L
A
I
N
S

MINNESOTA

Little Missouri River

B
A
D
L
A
N
D
S

Heart River

Cannonball River

Missouri
River

DRIFT
PRAIRIE

NORTH DAKOTA
Physical Map

Elevation

| 13000 | 10000 | 6000 | 3000 | 1800 | 600 | 0 Feet |
| 4000 | 3000 | 1800 | 900 | 550 | 200 | 0 Meters |

– – – State boundary

– · – International boundary

SOUTH DAKOTA

| 0 | 20 | 40 Miles |

| 0 | 20 | 40 | 60 | 80 Kilometers |

WYOMING

N
W   E
S

9

Three geographic regions define the land of North Dakota. The Red River Valley stretches along the state's eastern border. The Drift Prairie runs north to south through the middle of the state, and the Missouri Plateau spreads over most of western North Dakota.

A giant lake called Agassiz once covered the Red River Valley region. The lake was formed when **glaciers,** enormous, slow-moving sheets of ice, carved a huge hollow in the ground during the last

The Red River Valley in the eastern part of North Dakota offers rich soil for farming.

ice age. Water from melting glaciers and from nearby rivers filled up the giant hollow. The lake dried up thousands of years ago, leaving flat land and rich soil behind. The Red River Valley provides fertile ground for North Dakota farmers' crops.

The Drift Prairie is **pothole** country. As glaciers passed over the region, they scooped out thousands of small, shallow basins. Rain then filled them up, creating little lakes known as potholes.

Potholes (small lakes) often fill with water after heavy rains and dry up during hot periods.

North Dakota's colorful Badlands are a popular place to visit.

Most of the Drift Prairie region is **prairie,** or grassland. The prairie soil is very rich. When the glaciers melted, they left behind thick layers of **drift,** a mixture of clay, sand, and gravel, which made good dirt. Much of North Dakota's wheat, the state's most important crop, is grown on the Drift Prairie.

The Missouri Plateau is part of a **plateau** (highland) called the Great Plains, which stretches all the way from Canada to Texas. North Dakota's ranchers graze their cattle on the grasslands of the Missouri Plateau. Workers also mine the rich deposits of oil and coal that lie underneath the ground in this region.

In the southwestern part of the Missouri Plateau are the lonely **buttes,** or steep hills that stand alone, of the Badlands. Wind and water have carved these rocky hills into unusual shapes. Minerals in the rock add colorful bands of brown, red, and yellow to the buttes. Small streams flow around the buttes in this region. The streams flow toward North Dakota's larger rivers.

The Missouri River—the second-longest river in the United States—winds its way south across western North Dakota. The river is sometimes called Big Muddy because of all the mud in its water. The Little Missouri, Heart, and Cannonball Rivers flow into the Missouri River.

Along North Dakota's eastern border, the Red River heads north into Canada. The Sheyenne and several smaller rivers drain into the Red River.

Many small lakes dot North Dakota's Drift Prairie region. Devils Lake is the largest natural lake in the state. But Lake Sakakawea, an artificial lake, is bigger. It was formed when the Garrison Dam was built to collect floodwaters on the Missouri River.

Long, cold winters and short, hot summers are common in North Dakota. Wind blows blizzards into the state in the winter and brings heat waves in the summer. Temperatures average 70° F in summer and only 7° F in winter. During the winter, the state gets about 32 inches of snow.

Winter frost turns trees and grasses along the Missouri River white.

North Dakota is one of the driest states in the country. Some western parts of the state receive only about 13 inches of **precipitation** (rain and melted snow) each year. Farmers in the

North Dakota's state flower is the wild prairie rose *(above)*. The state's western plains are home to the mule deer *(right)*.

eastern part of the state, though, can usually count on getting about 20 inches.

Because of its dry weather, North Dakota does not have many trees. Only about 1 percent of the land is forested, mostly with aspen, poplar, white pine, cedar, and cottonwood. In spring and summer, the prairie comes alive with the bright blossoms of pasqueflowers, coneflowers, and red lilies. Chokecherries, highbush cranberries, and wild plums ripen on the grasslands.

White-tailed deer roam throughout the state. In the Badlands, prairie dogs dig their underground homes. Mule deer and pronghorn antelope leap among the rocks and crags. One of North Dakota's nicknames—the Flickertail State—comes from the flickertail squirrels that make their homes in the central part of the state.

Huge herds of bison, or buffalo, once grazed on North Dakota's prairie, but millions were killed by hunters in the 1800s. The U.S. government later passed laws to protect bison, and their numbers have since grown.

Natives and Newcomers

The first people to live in what later became North Dakota were hunters. They came to the area more than 10,000 years ago, when glaciers still covered most of North America. The hunters probably crossed a land bridge, which once connected Asia to North America. They were stalking animals such as mammoths—huge creatures that looked like hairy elephants. The descendants of these hunters, called Indians or Native Americans, eventually settled throughout North America.

Around the year 400 B.C., groups of people moved to North Dakota from the forests of what later became Minnesota and Wisconsin. Named Woodland Indians by historians, these people lived in villages along the rivers of eastern North Dakota and built houses of branches, grasses, bark, and animal hides. The Woodland Indians hunted deer and buffalo and grew corn and squash.

North Dakota's first inhabitants probably followed herds of mammoths to the area. These early people hunted mammoths for food.

After A.D. 600, hunters began to follow herds of buffalo across the plains of the area that became western North Dakota. These hunters, who may have been descendants of earlier Woodland Indians, are known as Plains Indians. Always on the move, these Plains Indians lived in tepees, which were easy to put up and take down.

Other Plains Indians made more permanent homes near the Missouri River. Among these were the Mandan. The Mandan moved west from the Mississippi River valley in A.D. 1000. They settled along the Missouri River in the area that became North Dakota. Later, the Hidatsa and Arikara settled near the Mandan.

The Mandan, Hidatsa, and Arikara lived in permanent villages of earthern homes. As many as 1,200 people lived in

Large circles of stone—called tepee rings—held tepees in place.

these villages. For protection, each village was surrounded by a ditch and a wall of wooden posts. In nearby fields, residents grew corn, beans, squash, and sunflowers. These Indians also hunted buffalo, eating the meat and using the hides for clothes and the bones for tools.

In about 1700, the Ojibway Indians drove their enemies, the Dakota, or Sioux, out of central Minnesota. The Dakota made new homes in the Drift Prairie region of what later became North Dakota. The state takes its name from these Indians. *Dakota* means "allies" or "friends" in their language.

Mandan women made bullboats by stretching buffalo hides over frames of willow tree branches. The buffalo's tail was left on to mark the back of the boat. Large bullboats could hold as many as eight people.

The first European to visit the area that later became North Dakota was a French Canadian fur trader named Pierre de La Vérendrye. He walked from Manitoba, Canada, to North Dakota in 1738, setting up fur-trading posts along the way. British, French, and Spanish fur traders soon followed.

These traders gave metal pots, glass beads, cloth, and guns to the Indians in exchange for buffalo hides and meat. White traders wanted beaver furs, too, which were popular in Europe for making hats.

The traders also carried diseases such as smallpox, cholera, measles, and tuberculosis. Native Americans had never been exposed to these illnesses before. Their bodies were unable to fight the diseases and thousands died.

Pierre de La Vérendrye was the first European to visit the North Dakota area.

Many thousands of Native Americans died of smallpox and other diseases brought by European traders. This picture shows the Dakota tradition of raising their dead on platforms above the ground to dry. The bones of the dead were later buried.

In the search for furs and other riches, European nations gradually claimed much of the land on which Native Americans made their homes. The French, for example, claimed a huge area that stretched all the way from the Mississippi River to the Rocky Mountains. Almost all of what later became North Dakota was part of this claim, called the Louisiana Territory. France sold the Louisiana Territory to the United States in 1803.

In the spring of 1804, U.S. president Thomas Jefferson sent explorers Meriwether Lewis and William Clark to map the new territory. Lewis and Clark traveled by canoe up the Missouri River from Saint Louis, Missouri. In the fall, the explorers arrived at the villages of the Mandan and the Hidatsa in central North Dakota. Lewis and Clark built Fort Mandan to live in until spring.

While at Fort Mandan, Lewis and Clark met Sacagawea, a young Shoshone Indian woman. In April 1805, Sacagawea joined the expedition. She guided the group, helping bring it safely to the Pacific Coast and back again.

Sacagawea met explorers Lewis and Clark in 1804 and later joined their expedition.

In the 1800s, some fur traders followed the Red River to Saint Paul, Minnesota, where they exchanged their goods for manufactured products. Wagons known as Red River carts were loaded with buffalo robes and furs.

In 1812 Thomas Douglas, a Scottish nobleman, brought a group of Scottish and Irish **immigrants** (newcomers) to North America. They settled near two important fur-trading posts in what later became the northeastern corner of North Dakota. The immigrants grew food for the trappers and traders. The immigrants' new town, Pembina, was North Dakota's first white settlement.

By 1830 North Dakota had many trading posts. Native Americans came with furs to Fort Union and Fort Clark on the Missouri River. Steamboats carried the furs down the river to Saint Louis and returned with manufactured goods to be traded for more furs.

As pioneers moved to the West, the U.S. government created territories out of the land they settled. A territory did not have as much power as a state, but with enough people, a territory could apply for statehood. In 1861 the U.S. government established the Dakota Territory. The territory included the areas that became North and South Dakota and much of Montana and Wyoming.

The U.S. government offered free land in the Dakota Territory. Many pioneers packed up their belongings in covered wagons and moved to the region.

To encourage more white settlers to move to the new territory, the United States offered free land to those who would live on it and improve it. At first, few settlers came to the Dakota Territory because it was difficult to travel that far west. Trains did not go as far as the Dakota Territory. Travel by covered wagon was slow. On such a long journey across the isolated prairies, sickness and injury often meant death.

Over time, more and more white people faced the dangers and moved into the Dakota Territory. As these settlers moved farther and farther west, they forced Native Americans off the land. The U.S. government made **treaties**, or agreements, allowing Native Americans to keep some land. But the government often broke the treaties, claiming more land for white settlers.

As white people settled in nearby Minnesota, many Native Americans moved west to the Dakota Territory, looking for new homes. Other Native Americans tried to fight for their land. Several battles between Native Americans and the U.S.

Army were fought in the southern part of North Dakota.

By the late 1860s, the U.S. government had established **reservations,** or areas of land set aside for Native Americans. By 1870 the Dakota, the Mandan, the Hidatsa, and the Arikara were living on reservations in the Dakota Territory.

Dakota women pose for a photograph in front of their tepees, near Fort Totten. The site later became the Devil's Lake Sioux (Dakota) Reservation.

Once the Native Americans were on reservations, railroad companies quickly built tracks across the Dakota Territory. Railroad companies wanted settlers to build homes and plant crops near the tracks. Then the settlers would buy train tickets when they needed to travel, and they would pay the railroads to ship crops to market.

Huge farms required large numbers of workers, horses, and machinery.

One way railroad companies thought they could attract people was to help set up big, successful farms. In 1875 the Northern Pacific Railroad asked a man named Oliver Dalrymple to manage a 13,000-acre wheat farm west of the city of Fargo. Dalrymple, known as the Minnesota Wheat King, accepted the offer and sold his wheat farm in Minnesota. His new

North Dakota farm was very successful.

Hearing of Dalrymple's success, other rich people set up even bigger wheat farms in the Dakota Territory. Some were four times the size of Dalrymple's farm. Hundreds of men, horses, and machines were required to do all the work. Because these farms were so big and made so much money, they were called bonanza farms.

Colorful posters advertised railroad service to the Dakota Territory.

The railroad companies were right. Stories of the bonanza farms attracted many people to the eastern Dakota Territory in the 1870s and 1880s. To attract even more settlers, the railroad companies went to northern Europe to advertise inexpensive farmland in the Dakota Territory. They also advertised in newspapers across the United States and in Canada.

In the 1880s, thousands of Norwegians and Germans came to the Dakota Territory. Many Canadians came to farm, too. So did people from New York, Minnesota, Wisconsin, and Iowa.

As the railroads laid tracks farther west, people followed. Many started ranches. Cowboys drove cattle into the Dakota Territory from faraway Colorado and Texas. Cattle thrived on the prairie grasses in the western Dakota Territory.

Before long, however, too many cattle were grazing on the prairie. They stripped the land of its valuable grasses. The summer of 1886 was extremely hot and dry. Prairie fires destroyed even more grass.

By the time winter came, thousands of cattle were starving. Already very weak, many cows froze to death. Disappointed and penniless, some of the ranchers left the Dakota Territory.

Many North Dakota settlers built their houses out of sod (blocks of dirt and grass). Few trees grew in North Dakota and lumber was scarce.

Medora

The Marquis de Mores with his wife, Medora, for whom the settlement in the Badlands was named

One of North Dakota's most famous ranchers was a French nobleman, the Marquis de Mores. In 1883 the marquis came to North Dakota's Badlands with a new idea. Instead of sending North Dakota's cattle to be butchered in Eastern cities, the marquis wanted to butcher the cattle in North Dakota. The meat could then be shipped to market more easily than live cattle could.

To test his idea, the marquis built a town and named it after his wife, Medora. The marquis set up a ranch to raise cattle and sheep and to breed horses. He built a meat-packing plant, where the cattle would be butchered. The marquis also built a church and a school.

Many ranchers followed and Medora boomed. But the marquis didn't stay long. Drought and fire in 1886 killed the grass on which cattle depended for food. Thousands of cattle starved to death, and many ranchers in the area—including the marquis—gave up their operations. By 1889 Medora had been abandoned.

Despite the troubles faced by ranchers, many people stayed. By the late 1800s, more than 500,000 people lived in the Dakota Territory—enough to apply for statehood. But since most railroad tracks ran across the territory from east to west, people in the northern and southern parts of the Dakota Territory had little contact with each other. For that reason, the Dakota Territory was split in half. On November 2, 1889, North Dakota became the 39th state and South Dakota the 40th.

North Dakota's population grew quickly as railroads continued to build tracks in the state. Towns sprang up near the railroad tracks. In 1890 more than 190,000 people lived in North Dakota. By 1910 the state's population had grown to more than 500,000.

The 1920s were hard years for North Dakotans. Prices for crops were low. Little rain fell, and crops did poorly. Wheat prices dropped still lower in the 1930s, and dry weather continued. Grass didn't grow, so cattle starved. Dust storms blew away the dry topsoil, and huge swarms of grasshoppers ate almost everything that survived the **drought.**

A North Dakota farmer scans the skies for rain.

The Nonpartisan League

In the early 1900s, many of North Dakota's farmers were dissatisfied. The main offices of the railroads that carried North Dakota's crops to market were in Minnesota. So were the banks that lent money to North Dakota's farmers. The grain companies that bought North Dakota's wheat were also in Minnesota. North Dakota' farmers wanted more control. They wanted to have their own banks and their own grain companies.

In 1915 Arthur C. Townley, a North Dakota farmer, organized a group called the Nonpartisan League to help farmers. Townley traveled across the state talking to farmers about their problems. Farmers joined the league in large numbers, and by 1916 the league had about 40,000 members and its own newspaper. With so many members, the league was very powerful. The league's leaders urged North Dakota's government to make changes to help the state's farmers.

In 1919 the state government opened the Bank of North Dakota in the city of Bismarck. By 1922 the state had opened its own grain elevator in Grand Forks, which stored grain at lower prices than the Minnesota elevators did. Both the bank and the elevator are still in operation.

Arthur C. Townley speaks to a crowd at Johannes Farm near Steele, North Dakota.

The Garrison Dam was built in the 1940s and 1950s. The creation of the dam flooded 155,000 acres of farmland that belonged to the Mandan, Hidatsa, and Arikara.

During World War II (1939–1945), economic conditions for North Dakota's farmers improved. Prices for crops and cattle were high because these products were needed to help feed U.S. troops. With better weather, crops were healthy and farmers made a lot of money.

In 1946, after terrible floods along the Missouri River, North Dakotans began building the Garrison Dam. The dam, which took 14 years to build, prevents floods by holding excess rainwater in an artificial lake. Water from the lake is then released in powerful streams that turn engines. These engines create electricity for homes and businesses in North Dakota.

The U.S. government created many jobs in 1957 when it built an air force base in Minot, North Dakota. In 1960 a second base, in Grand Forks, was completed. These bases train pilots and shelter bombers.

More jobs and money came to North Dakota with the discovery of oil in the western part of the state. By the 1970s, oil had become an important industry. Many North Dakotans earned money by pumping and refining this energy-producing mineral.

A statue of a buffalo stands on the grounds of North Dakota's capitol, a skyscraper in Bismarck.

Most North Dakotans still rely on agriculture and related services to make a living. Since earnings from farms can be unpredictable, North Dakotans are looking for ways to bring different kinds of jobs to the state.

The Sacagawea gold dollar coin

In 1997 massive flooding in eastern North Dakota caused millions of dollars in damage. Almost the entire city of Grand Forks was flooded. Nearly all of the city's 60,000 people had to be evacuated. North Dakotans worked together in recovery efforts and in creating new plans to deal with flooding.

In the year 2000, the U.S. government honored one North Dakotan—Sacagawea —in a special way. The U.S. Mint created a gold dollar coin with her image on it. North Dakotans continue to value their heritage and their tradition of hard work.

Living Off the Land

Pioneers arriving in North Dakota came to farm the rich prairie soil or to graze cattle on the western plains. More than 100 years later, about half of North Dakota's 642,200 residents still live on farms or in small towns.

Only four of North Dakota's cities have more than 25,000 people. About 91,000 people live in Fargo, the largest city. Bismarck is the state capital. Grand Forks is home to the University of North Dakota, and Minot is the site of a U.S. Air Force base.

Huge clouds form over the prairies of Stark County *(left)*. A rancher rounds up a herd of horses *(opposite page)*.

About 92 percent of North Dakotans are descendants of settlers who came in the 1800s. Most of their ancestors came from Norway or Germany. In addition, many North Dakotans have ancestors who immigrated from Canada. Native Americans make up about 5 percent of the state's population. North Dakota also has small numbers of Latinos, African Americans, and Asian Americans.

North Dakotans have often looked to their own people for entertainment. The state has many

Many North Dakotans are descendants of Europeans.

The Dakota Cowboy Poetry Gathering attracts tourists from near and far.

community theater groups, including the Little Country Theater in Fargo. Minot, Fargo, and Grand Forks each sponsor a symphony orchestra.

Every Memorial Day weekend, the town of Medora holds the Dakota Cowboy Poetry Gathering, where cowboy poets from around the country recite their verses. Every July, Dickinson hosts the Roughrider Days Rodeo. The Mandan, Hidatsa, Arikara, Ojibway, and Dakota celebrate their heritage at the United Tribes Powwow, held each September in Bismarck.

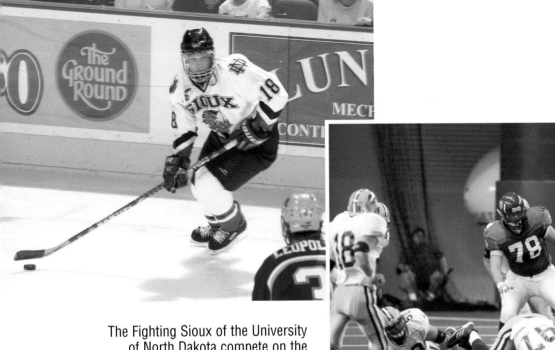

The Fighting Sioux of the University of North Dakota compete on the ice *(above).* The Bison football team (dark jerseys) plays for North Dakota State University *(right).*

North Dakota has no professional sports teams. But residents enjoy watching their state's college teams. The University of North Dakota's hockey team, the Fighting Sioux, has won several national championships. North Dakota State University's football team, the Bison, has also succeeded at the national level.

Throughout the year, North Dakotans enjoy the outdoors. They go boating and fishing on Devils Lake or Lake Sakakawea. Many people picnic and camp at Lake Metigoshe State Park, one of North Dakota's 18 state parks and recreation areas. Animal lovers watch eagles, antelope, and bison in Theodore Roosevelt National Park.

The Cannonball River is a great place for canoeing.

Many North Dakota farmers grow
wheat *(below)* and raise cattle *(left).*

North Dakota earns more money from agriculture than most other states do. The state has close to 31,000 farms and ranches. About 90 percent of North Dakota's land is used either for grazing cattle or for growing crops.

Wheat is North Dakota's major crop. In fact, only Kansas grows more wheat than North Dakota. Some of North Dakota's farmers plant a special variety of wheat called durum. Durum wheat is used to make spaghetti and other pastas.

Flax is used to make linen. It is also grown for its seeds.

North Dakota's farmers plant many other crops as well. The state ranks first in growing barley, sunflowers, and flax. Linseed oil, which is used to make paint, comes from crushed flaxseeds. Oats, rye, and sugar beets are also important crops in the state.

North Dakota's farmers grow hay to feed the state's cattle. Ranchers raise beef and dairy cattle. Because hogs like to eat corn, most pigs are found on farms in the eastern part of the state, where corn grows well. North Dakotans also raise sheep and poultry.

Service workers include waiters and waitresses.

Almost two-thirds of North Dakota's workers have jobs that provide a service to others. The people who sell equipment to farmers have service jobs. So do the bankers who help farmers get loans. Some service workers have jobs in restaurants. Other North Dakotans work in government offices. The people who work at the U.S. Air Force bases in Minot and Grand Forks have government jobs, too.

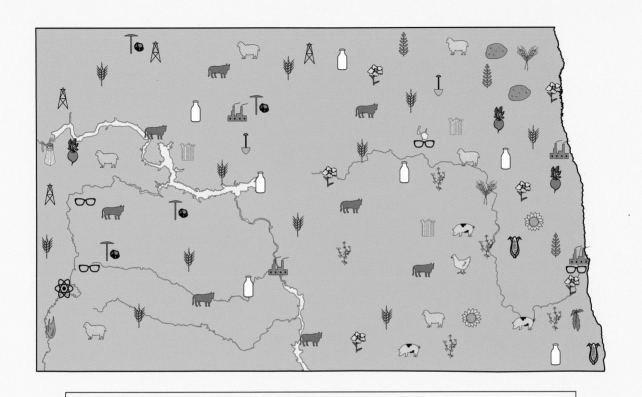

NORTH DAKOTA
Economic Map

The symbols on this map show where different economic activities take place in North Dakota. The legend below explains what each symbol stands for.

Symbol		Symbol		Symbol	
Barley	Flax	Milk	Potatoes	Sand and gravel	Sunflowers
Beef cattle	Hay	Natural gas	Poultry	Sheep	Tourism
Coal	Hogs	Oats	Rye	Soybeans	Uranium
Corn	Manufacturing	Oil	Salt	Sugar beets	Wheat

North Dakota has few manufacturing jobs because many companies can't afford the high cost of transporting goods from the state to markets in distant cities. Most of the 25,000 North Dakotans who have manufacturing jobs process food from the crops and livestock that farmers provide. Workers at plants in Dickinson and Finley make frozen bread dough. Many people have jobs at meat-packing plants in Fargo. Sugar is processed from sugar beets at

Minot is home to a large air force base.

refineries in Grand Forks, Hillsboro, and Wahpeton.

Some North Dakotans make a living by taking minerals from the earth. Oil is pumped from underground oil fields in western North Dakota. Later it is cleaned and processed into gasoline at an oil refinery in Mandan in the southern part of the state.

Other miners dig the state's deposits of coal, some of which are found in the Badlands. The coal is then burned at power plants to produce electricity. North Dakotans also dig for clay, which is used to make bricks and ceramics. Road construction crews depend upon the state's sand and gravel to build roads.

Oil was discovered in North Dakota in 1951. It earns the state more money than any other mineral.

Preserving the Wetlands

North Dakota's wetlands—which include potholes, bogs, marshes, swamps, and the shorelines of rivers and lakes—provide food, water, and shelter for many animals and plants. Salamanders and frogs live in wetlands. Plants that need lots of water, such as the prairie fringed orchid and the marsh fern, grow in wetlands.

Muskrats dig their burrows into the banks of streams. A small, sand-colored bird called the piping plover makes its nest on the sandbars of the Missouri River. In the spring, between 2 and 3 million ducklings hatch in North Dakota's potholes.

Prairie fringed orchid

Potholes offer migrating ducks and geese places to rest.

North Dakota's wildlife refuges have been set aside for plants and animals to live undisturbed by humans.

But potholes and other wetlands in North Dakota are disappearing. More than half of the state's original wetlands are gone. Farmers drain wetlands or fill them up with dirt to create more land for growing crops. Workers drain wetlands in places where they need more solid ground for building roads, houses, and stores.

As North Dakota's wetlands vanish, so do plants and animals. Plants that need marshy areas to survive die when their watery habitats, or homes, are drained. Animals lose safe places to make their homes. Wetland grasses, for example, offer protection for ducks and their chicks. When a duck's wetland nesting site disappears, the duck is forced to move to an area where it may not be safe from predators such as foxes.

Wetlands offer more than a safe place for animals to make their homes. North Dakota's potholes, for example, help control pollution. After a heavy rain, harmful chemicals that people use to kill weeds and insects sometimes wash into potholes. Water in potholes moves slowly, so the chemicals have time to settle to the bottom. This makes water that runs out of the potholes and into nearby lakes and streams less polluted.

Many mallard ducks make their homes in North Dakota's wildlife refuges.

Dry potholes fill up with rainwater after storms. This helps to prevent nearby rivers from flooding.

Potholes also act as dams that control floods. When heavy rain falls, or when snow melts in the spring, potholes fill up and hold this water. The water then trickles away slowly or eventually dries up. Because the potholes hold extra water, nearby streams and rivers are less likely to overflow and flood the surrounding land.

The people of North Dakota are finding ways to save their wetlands. In 1987 the state passed a law requiring landowners who plan to drain 80 acres or more of wetlands to apply for a permit from the state. If the permit is granted, the landowner may drain the wetlands but must also help pay to replace the same amount of wetlands elsewhere in the state. This way, North Dakota will not lose any more of its valuable wetlands.

A photographer takes shots of Lostwood National Wildlife Refuge, a protected wetland area in North Dakota.

Willet live and nest in North Dakota's wetlands. Without this natural resource, these birds may become extinct.

North Dakota and the U.S. governments are also working together to save the wetlands. In some cases, the U.S. government buys wetlands and the surrounding land to make sure private owners do not drain or fill them. In other cases, the U.S. government pays North Dakota's farmers to leave wetlands alone when they are filled with water. During dry periods, farmers may plant crops or graze cattle in the dry wetlands.

A number of programs actually pay North Dakota landowners to restore and maintain wetlands. The North Dakota Wildlife Extension Program pays landowners to create wetlands on their property. The North Dakota Waterbank Program pays residents to maintain the wetlands they currently own.

Despite these programs, many farmers would still make more money if they turned their wetlands into cropland. But North Dakotans understand the importance of their environment and enjoy their state's natural beauty. They are willing to make less money now so that future generations can enjoy the state's wilderness, too.

Fun Facts

Jamestown, North Dakota, is home to the World's Largest Buffalo. The statue, which stands on a hilltop, weighs 60 tons.

The Red River, in eastern North Dakota, is one of the rare rivers in the world that flows northward.

On November 2, 1889, President Benjamin Harrison signed the documents that made North and South Dakota the 39th and 40th states. The president covered the papers before signing them, so no one knows which Dakota became a state first. But since North Dakota comes first alphabetically, it is officially known as the 39th state.

World's Largest Buffalo in Jamestown

The geographic center of North America lies near Rugby, North Dakota, 45 miles south of the Canadian border.

More ducks make their nests in North Dakota than in any other state except Alaska.

Sometimes, when lightning strikes or when dry prairie grasses catch fire in the Badlands of North Dakota, the ground cracks open and the coal underneath catches fire. The coal can burn for many years, hardening the ground and turning it brick red.

The International Peace Garden near Dunseith, North Dakota, lies partly in the United States and partly in Canada. The flowers and trees in the park stand for the long friendship between the two countries.

North Dakota borders three U.S. states and two Canadian provinces. Minnesota lies to the east, South Dakota to the south, Montana to the west. The Canadian provinces of Saskatchewan and Manitoba lie to the north.

STATE SONG

North Dakota's state song was written in 1926 and
officially adopted the next year.

NORTH DAKOTA HYMN

Words by James W. Foley; music by Dr. C. S. Putnam

You can hear "North Dakota Hymn" by visiting this website:
<http://www.50states.com/songs/ndakota.htm>

A NORTH DAKOTA RECIPE

North Dakota is a leading producer of durum wheat. Durum wheat is used to make semolina, a kind of flour that is used to make pasta. Try this recipe to make fresh pasta, in any style or shape you like. Having a pasta machine to make your favorite shape will help but is not necessary. Be sure to ask for an adult's help with all steps involving boiling water.

EASY FRESH PASTA

2 cups all-purpose flour
2 cups semolina flour
1 pinch salt

6 large eggs
2 tablespoons olive oil

1. Sift together all-purpose flour, semolina, and salt. Make mound of this mixture. Make a well in center of mound. Break eggs and olive oil into well. Beat eggs very gently with fork, gradually mixing in flour.
2. After a while, mixture will become too hard to mix with fork. Use your hands to knead dough until it is smooth, about 8 to 12 minutes.
3. Dust dough with flour to keep it from becoming too sticky. Wrap dough in plastic. Let rest at room temperature for 30 minutes.
4. Roll out dough to desired thickness with rolling pin or pasta-making machine. Cut into your favorite style of noodle.
5. Bring water to boil in large pot. Add 4 teaspoons of salt. Cook pasta until tender but not mushy. (The amount of cooking time needed for this will depend on your pasta's thickness.)
6. Drain pasta in colander and serve with your favorite sauce.

Makes eight servings.

HISTORICAL TIMELINE

8,000 B.C. Native Americans come to the region that later becomes North Dakota.

400 B.C. Woodland Indians settle in eastern North Dakota.

A.D. 600 Plains Indians roam the plains of North Dakota, hunting buffalo.

1000 Mandan Indians settle along the Missouri River.

1700 Dakota Indians move to North Dakota from Minnesota.

1738 Pierre de la Vérendrye travels through North Dakota.

1804 Meriwether Lewis and William Clark build Fort Mandan.

1812 Thomas Douglas brings Scottish and Irish immigrants to Pembina, creating North Dakota's first permanent white settlement.

1861 The U.S. government establishes the Dakota Territory.

1870 The Dakota, Mandan, Hidatsa, and Arikara Indians are living on reservations in the Dakota Territory.

1875 Oliver Dalrymple begins managing the first bonanza farm.

1889 North Dakota becomes the 39th state.

1891 North Dakota's population reaches more than 500,000.

1920s Crop prices fall; many North Dakota farms go bankrupt.

1939–1945 North Dakota crops contribute to the war efforts of the United States and its allies during World War II.

1946 Construction of the Garrison Dam begins.

1951 Oil is discovered in western North Dakota.

1957 A U.S. Air Force base is built in Minot.

1960 The Garrison Dam is completed; a U.S. Air Force base is built in Grand Forks.

1989 The state of North Dakota celebrates its centennial.

1997 Record floods devastate the Red River Valley.

OUTSTANDING NORTH DAKOTANS

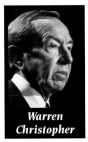

James Buchli

Warren Christopher

Ronald Davies

Lynn Anderson (born 1947) is a country-western singer who recorded such hit songs as "Rose Garden" and "Top of the World," which became popular in the 1970s. Anderson is originally from Grand Forks.

James Buchli (born 1945) is an astronaut who has been a crew member on several space voyages. In 1985 he was a flight engineer on the *Discovery* satellite-launching mission. The same year, Buchli was part of the *Challenger* crew for a Spacelab mission. In 1989 he again flew with *Discovery*. Buchli grew up in Fargo.

Warren Christopher (born 1925) served as U.S. secretary of state from 1993 to 1997. His accomplishments in this position included assisting in the creation of a peace agreement in Bosnia and the reorganization of the U.S. State Department. Christopher also served as deputy secretary of state from 1977 to 1981. In this role, he helped to free the U.S. hostages held in Iran. Christopher was born in Scranton, North Dakota.

Ronald Davies (1904–1996) was a judge from Grand Forks who became famous when he was called to fill in for a federal judge in Little Rock, Arkansas, in 1957. Davies's first task in Arkansas was to enforce the famous U.S. Supreme Court decision to allow black students and white students to attend the same public schools.

Angie Dickinson (born 1931) grew up in Edgeley, North Dakota. In the 1970s, she starred in the TV series *Police Woman*. Dickinson has also been in many movies, including *Dressed to Kill* and *Even Cowgirls Get the Blues*.

Angie Dickinson

Richard Edlund (born 1940) of Fargo is a special-effects technician. His work appears in several films, including *Star Wars, Poltergeist, Ghostbusters, Alien 3,* and *Air Force One.* Edlund has won several Academy Awards.

Richard Edlund

Louise Erdrich (born 1954) is a poet and the author of many short stories and novels. Erdrich and the late author Michael Dorris wrote *The Crown of Columbus,* a novel about the search for the lost journal of Christopher Columbus. Erdrich grew up in Wahpeton, North Dakota, and is a member of the Turtle Mountain Band of Chippewa.

Louise Erdrich

Phyllis Frelich (born 1944), a deaf actress, is one of the founding members of the National Theater of the Deaf. She has appeared in many plays, including the popular Broadway production of *Children of a Lesser God,* for which she won a Tony Award. Frelich is from Devils Lake, North Dakota.

Phyllis Frelich

Virgil Hill (born 1963), a boxer, grew up in Grand Forks. Hill has won the Golden Gloves and the North American boxing titles, as well as a silver medal in the 1984 Olympic Games. In 1987 he won the World Boxing Association's light heavyweight title, which he defended until 1990.

Phil Jackson (born 1945) is one of the most successful coaches in the history of the National Basketball Association. One of Jackson's teams, the Chicago Bulls, won six championships in eight seasons in the 1990s. Jackson has continued this success as coach of the Los Angeles Lakers, winning championships in 2000 and 2001. Jackson also played in the NBA for 13 seasons. He grew up in Williston.

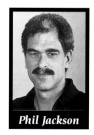

Phil Jackson

Louis L'Amour

Peggy Lee

Roger Maris

Lute Olson

Louis L'Amour (1908–1988) wrote more million-copy bestselling books than any other American writer of fiction. His many action-packed novels, short stories, and film and television scripts are known for their realistic descriptions of life in the Old West. Some of his dozens of novels include *The Walking Drum*, *Last of the Breed*, and *Sackett*. L'Amour was born in Jamestown, North Dakota.

Peggy Lee (1920–2002) was from Jamestown, North Dakota. As a singer, she toured with Benny Goodman's band, going on to record with stars such as Bing Crosby and Jimmy Durante. Lee wrote and sang much of the music for the animated film *Lady and the Tramp* and starred in two motion pictures—*The Jazz Singer* and *Pete Kelly's Blues*.

Roger Maris (1934–1985), of Fargo, was one of major league baseball's greatest sluggers of the 1960s. Playing right field for the New York Yankees, he won the American League's Most Valuable Player Award in 1960 and 1961. In 1961 Maris hit 61 home runs—the all-time single season record at that time. His record stood until 1998.

Casper Oimoen (1906–1995), raised in Minot, was a champion ski jumper. He competed in the 1932 and 1936 Winter Olympic Games and won over 400 medals and trophies in his ski jumping career. Oimoen was elected to the U.S. Skiing Hall of Fame in 1963.

Lute Olson (born 1935) is one of the winningest coaches in NCAA Division I men's basketball history. Olson has had more than 600 wins in Division I, as well as five Final Four appearances, and a National Championship in 1997. The majority of Olson's wins have come as coach of the University of Arizona Wildcats, the team he has coached since 1983. Olson was born in Maryville.

James Rosenquist (born 1933) was a key member of the pop art movement of the 1960s that included Andy Warhol, Claes Oldenburg, and Jasper Johns. His most famous painting is of a U.S. warplane. Entitled *F-111*, the painting is actually larger than the plane it was named after. Rosenquist was born in Grand Forks.

James Rosenquist

Sacagawea (1786?–1812), a Shoshone Indian, was captured by Hidatsa Indians as a child. She later married a French Canadian trader named Toussaint Charbonneau. Sacagawea, also known as Sakakawea, and her husband accompanied the Lewis and Clark expedition west from North Dakota, helping as guides and interpreters.

Eric Sevareid

Eric Sevareid (1912–1992) began his journalism career as a newspaper reporter and went on to become one of the most well-known faces of television news. Born in Velva, North Dakota, Sevareid was a news correspondent for CBS during World War II and later appeared regularly on the *CBS Evening News.*

Era Bell Thompson (1905–1987) moved to Driscoll, North Dakota, with her family as a child. Thompson studied at the University of North Dakota and went on to publish several books, including *Africa, Land of My Fathers*, and *White on Black.* In 1947 she joined *Ebony* magazine, for which she became the international editor.

Era Bell Thompson

Lawrence Welk (1903–1992), from Strasburg, North Dakota, was one of America's most beloved TV personalities. Welk formed a band in the 1920s and became popular in the 1950s as the bandleader and host of TV's *The Lawrence Welk Show*, which ran from 1955 to 1982. Welk was known as the King of Champagne Music.

Lawrence Welk

FACTS-AT-A-GLANCE

Nicknames: Flickertail State, Peace Garden State

Song: "North Dakota Hymn"

Motto: Liberty and Union Now and Forever, One and Inseparable

Flower: wild prairie rose

Tree: American elm

Bird: western meadowlark

Fish: northern pike

Fossil: teredo petrified wood

Grass: western wheatgrass

Beverage: milk

Date and ranking of statehood: November 2, 1889, the 39th state

Capital: Bismarck

Area: 68,994 square miles

Rank in area, nationwide: 17th

Average January temperature: 7° F

Average July temperature: 70° F

North Dakota's flag is based on a flag carried by the North Dakota Infantry in the Spanish American War. The bald eagle on North Dakota's flag is a U.S. symbol of freedom. North Dakota's eagle grasps seven arrows and an olive branch. The arrows symbolize strength, while the olive branch symbolizes peace.

POPULATION GROWTH

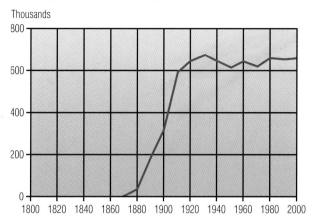

Thousands

This chart shows how North Dakota's population has changed from 1870 to 2000.

North Dakota's state seal shows a tree surrounded by wheat, a plow, an anvil, and a sledge. These objects represent agriculture. The Indian on horseback chasing a buffalo represents the Indian nations of North Dakota.

Population: 642,200 (2000 census)

Rank in population, nationwide: 47th

Major cities and populations: (2000 census) Fargo (90,599), Bismarck (55,532), Grand Forks (49,321), Minot (36,567), Mandan (16,718)

U.S. senators: 2

U.S. representatives: 1

Electoral votes: 3

Natural resources: clay, lignite coal, natural gas, petroleum, salt, sand and gravel, soil

Agricultural products: barley, canola, canola seed, flaxseed, hay, honey, sunflowers, wheat

Manufactured goods: food products, machinery, petroleum products, printed materials, transportation equipment

WHERE NORTH DAKOTANS WORK

Services—62 percent (services includes jobs in trade; community, social, and personal services; finance, insurance, and real estate; transportation, communication, and utilities)

Government—16 percent

Agriculture—10 percent

Manufacturing—6 percent

Construction—5 percent

Mining—1 percent

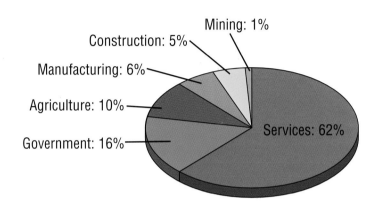

GROSS STATE PRODUCT

Services—56 percent

Agriculture—15 percent

Government—14 percent

Manufacturing—7 percent

Construction—5 percent

Mining—3 percent

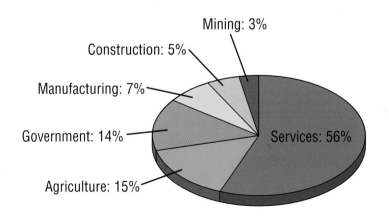

NORTH DAKOTA WILDLIFE

Mammals: American bison, beaver, chipmunk, coyote, lynx, mink, moose, porcupine, raccoon, red fox, skunk, squirrels, weasel, white-tailed deer, woodchuck

Birds: bald eagle, Baltimore oriole, blue jay, ducks, geese, great blue heron, northern cardinal, osprey, owls, pelican, red-tailed hawk, sparrows, waxwings, wild turkey

Amphibians and reptiles: eastern box turtle, eastern tiger salamander, garter snake, great plains toad, northern leopard frog, painted turtle, snapping turtle, western chorus frog

Fish: bass, bluegill, carp, catfish, crappie, perch, muskellunge, northern pike, trout

Trees: ash, aspen, basswood, box elder, cottonwood, elm, oak, poplar, willow

Wild plants: gumweed, juneberry, milkweed, pasqueflower, sarsaparilla, thimbleweed, wheatgrasses, wild strawberry, yarrow

Porcupine

Osprey

PLACES TO VISIT

Bonanzaville USA, West Fargo
This restored pioneer village has 40 museums covering 150 years of history. Visitors can see exhibits of antique farm machinery, antique cars, a railroad depot featuring a steam locomotive, a country school, a sod house, a bonanza farm home, and many other historical items.

Chateau de Mores State Historic Site, near Medora
Visit the winter home of the Marquis de Mores, founder of Medora. Take a guided tour of the 26-room mansion, and visit the interpretive center that includes artifacts from the 1800s.

Dakota Dinosaur Museum, Dickinson
This museum is home to a complete triceratops skelton and a duck-billed edmontosaurus fossil. It also houses ten other full-size dinosaurs. The museum features a collection of unique minerals as well.

Fort Abercrombie State Historic Site, near Wahpeton
Sioux Indians attacked this fort for six weeks in 1862. One original fort building remains, and the site features a museum that tells its history.

International Peace Garden, near Dunseith
Straddling the border of North Dakota and Manitoba, Canada, this 2,300-acre garden celebrates over 150 years of peace between the United States and its northern neighbor. In summer the gardens explode with the colors of over 140,000 flowers.

Knife River Indian Villages, near Bismarck

Visit one of the oldest inhabited sites in North America, which dates back at least 8,000 years. Trails lead to three different village sites. The visitor center features exhibits, audiovisual programs, books, and Native American crafts.

Lake Metigoshe State Park, near Bottineau

Camping, hiking, mountain biking, canoeing, fishing, sledding, picnicking, swimming, skiing, and snowmobiling are all available at this 1,500-acre park in the scenic Turtle Mountains. The park also features a National Recreation Trail.

Lewis and Clark National Historic Trail, Highways 1804 and 1806

Follow Lewis and Clark's historic journey along the Missouri River. Signs at different points along the way give details of the expedition. Travelers can follow the trail by road, or travel by canoe—just like Lewis and Clark.

Medora Doll House, Medora

Set in a historic home, the Medora Doll House features exhibits of dolls and toys from many different countries. Some of the dolls were made as long ago as the 1700s.

Theodore Roosevelt National Park, near Medora

This park is named after the country's 26th president, who lived in the region from 1884 until 1886. It includes 110 square miles of Badlands, some of the most colorful scenery in the world. The park is also home to herds of American bison and many other species of wildlife.

ANNUAL EVENTS

North Dakota Winter Show—*March*

Cowboy Poetry Gathering, Medora—*May*

Fort Union Trading Post Rendezvous, Williston—*June*

International Music Camp, International Peace Garden—*June–July*

Roughrider Days Rodeo, Dickinson—*July*

North Dakota State Fair, Minot—*July*

Pioneer Days at Bonanzaville, U.S.A., West Fargo—*August*

United Tribes International Powwow, Bismarck—*September*

Annual Gem and Mineral Show, Mandan—*September*

Norsk Hostfest, Minot—*October*

Threshing Bee, Makoti—*October*

Medora's Old Fashioned Cowboy Christmas, Medora—*December*

LEARN MORE ABOUT NORTH DAKOTA

BOOKS

General

Fradin, Dennis. *North Dakota.* Chicago: Children's Press, 1994.

Hintz, Martin. *North Dakota.* New York: Children's Press, 2000. For older readers.

McDaniel, Melissa. *North Dakota.* New York: Benchmark Books, 2001. For older readers.

Special Interest

Bial, Raymond. *The Sioux.* New York: Marshall Cavendish Corporation, 1999. For older readers. Read about the origins, beliefs, language, and culture of the Sioux, also known as the Dakota Indians.

Bowen, Andy Russell. *The Back of Beyond: A Story about Lewis and Clark.* Minneapolis, MN: Carolrhoda Books, Inc., 1997. Follow the adventures of Lewis and Clark as they explore the wilderness of the western United States.

St. George, Judith. *Sacagawea.* New York: G.P. Putnam's Sons, 1997. The story of the Shoshone Indian girl who helped guide the Lewis and Clark expedition of 1804–1806.

Toht, David W. *Sodbuster.* Minneapolis, MN: Lerner Publications Company, 1996. Explores the daily lives of settlers of the open plains in the early 1800s.

Fiction

Erdrich, Louise. *The Birchbark House.* New York: Hyperion Books for Children, 1999. Written by North Dakota native Louise Erdrich, this novel tells the story of Omakayas, a seven-year-old Native American girl of the Ojibway tribe, as she lives through the joys of summer and the perils of winter on an island on Lake Superior in 1847.

Kurtz, Jane. *Jakarta Missing.* New York: Greenwillow Books, 2001. Dakar longs for her home in Africa while adjusting to life in Cottonwood, North Dakota. She is also worried about her beloved sister Jakarta, who stayed behind in Africa.

WEBSITES

Discover ND: North Dakota's Source for State Government Information
<http://www.discovernd.com/>
The state of North Dakota's official website offers information on business, education, employment, government, health and safety, and law and order.

North Dakota Department of Tourism
<http://www.ndtourism.com/frames.html>
North Dakota's official tourism website features events, activities, attractions, and lodging in the state.

Bismarck Tribune Online
<http://www.bismarcktribune.com>
Follow current events in North Dakota with the online version of the capital city's newspaper.

PRONUNCIATION GUIDE

Agassiz (AG-uh-see)

Arikara (uh-RIHK-uh-ruh)

Dalrymple, Oliver (DAL-rihm-puhl, AHL-uh-vur)

Hidatsa (hih-DAHT-suh)

La Vérendrye, Pierre de (lah vay-rahn-DREE, pee-AIR duh)

Mandan (MAN-dan)

Minot (MY-naht)

Pembina (PEHM-buh-nuh)

Sacagawea (sah-KAH-gah-WEE-ah or SAK-uh-ja-WEE-ah)

Sheyenne (shy-EHN)

Sioux (SOO)

Wahpeton (WAW-puh-tuhn)

The Badlands are one of the most popular tourist attractions in North Dakota.

GLOSSARY

butte: an isolated hill or mountain with steep sides

drift: a mixture of clay, sand, and gravel deposited by a glacier, plus any materials added to this mixture by the running water of a melting glacier. Areas where drift has been deposited have very good soil for farming.

drought: a long period of extreme dryness due to lack of rain or snow

glacier: a large body of ice and snow that moves slowly over land

ice age: a period when ice sheets cover large regions of the earth

immigrant: a person who moves into a foreign country and settles there

plateau: a large, relatively flat area that stands above the surrounding land

pothole: a small depression in the land. After a rainstorm or when nearby snow melts, potholes fill up with water. In periods of hot and dry weather, the potholes often dry up.

prairie: a large area of level or gently rolling grassy land with few trees

precipitation: rain, snow, and other forms of moisture that fall to earth

reservation: public land set aside by the government to be used by Native Americans

treaty: an agreement between two or more groups, usually having to do with peace or trade

INDEX

PHOTO ACKNOWLEDGMENTS

Cover photographs by © Tom Bean/CORBIS (left); © Layne Kennedy/CORBIS (right); © Tom Bean/CORBIS, pp. 2–3; © Annie Griffiths Belt/CORBIS, p. 3; PhotoDisc, pp. 4, 7, 18, 40, 52; Craig Bihrle, North Dakota Game and Fish Department, pp. 6, 15, 16 (both), 51, 55; Utah DWR, p. 7; © Annie Griffiths Belt/CORBIS, pp. 10, 58; © Kent and Donna Dannen, pp. 11, 53; Lynda Richards, pp. 12, 46 (bottom), 47, 54; Smithsonian Institution photo #80-1819, p. 19; Independent Picture Service, pp. 21, 23, 60; State Historical Society of North Dakota, pp. 22, 25, 26, 29, 30–31, 32, 33, 34, 35, 36, 68 (top), 69 (second from bottom); Library of Congress, p. 27; © JeffGreenberg@juno.com, pp. 37, 38, 45, 48; Todd Strand/Independent Picture Service, pp. 39, 40 (left), 80; © Betty A. Kubis/Root Resources, p. 41; Cary Sukut, p. 42; © Sheldon Green/Library of Congress, p. 43; UND Athletic Department, p. 44 (both); © Craig Bihrle, p. 46 (inset); U.S. Air Force, p. 50; Linda Huhn, p. 52 (left); © Kirtley-Perkins/Visuals Unlimited, p. 56; © Tom Bean/CORBIS, p. 57; Jack Lindstrom, p. 61; NASA, p. 66 (top); © David & Peter Turnley/CORBIS, p. 66 (second from top); NDIRS-NDSU, Fargo, pp. 66 (second from bottom), 67 (second from bottom), 69 (second from top, bottom); Hollywood Book and Poster, pp. 66 (bottom), 68 (second from top); Boss Film Studios, p. 67 (top); Michael Dorris, p. 67 (second from top); Chicago Bulls, p. 67 (bottom); National Baseball Hall of Fame, p. 68 (second from bottom); © Reuters NewMedia Inc./CORBIS, p. 68 (bottom); © Richard Schulman/CORBIS, p. 69 (top); Jean Matheny, p. 70 (top); Minneapolis Public Library and Information Center, p. 73 (top); U.S. Fish and Wildlife Service, p. 73 (bottom).